POST AMERICA

A New Constitution

Don Durrett

(Third Edition, February 2026)

ISBN: 978-0-578-50102-4

WWW.DONDURRETT.COM

BOOKS BY DON DURRETT

The Demise of America

Kern County: The Path to Secession and a New Constitution

How to Invest in Gold and Silver: A Complete Guide with a Focus on Mining Stocks

America's Political Cold War

A Stranger From the Past

Conversations With an Immortal

Finding Your Soul

Your Soul Explained

Spirit Club

Last of the Gnostics

The Gathering

Ascension Training

Team Creator

A Republic, if you can keep it.

– Benjamin Franklin

CONTENTS

PREFACE

I originally wrote this new Constitution in 2018, and today it is 2026. I want to add some thoughts, so I'll stick them here in the preface.

I want to begin with the direction the country has been going in, which is clearly a road to ruin. We can begin with politics. Everything began to change (for the worse) right around when I was born in 1960. Prior to that time, America's values were pretty good and widely shared by most U.S. citizens. America was the envy of the world and widely respected as the world leader in freedom, economic strength, education, innovation, and human rights. We were looked towards as the country to emulate. At that time, our values were based on liberty (freedom), meritocracy (opportunity for high achievers), and the rule of law (following our Constitution). Political corruption was limited to a large extent, and people tried to do the right thing. It was a time of innocence.

In 1960, as a nation, we knew what was important, as reflected by our values. Moreover, we were all Americans, and we got along. I won't deny that racism was still prevalent, and women were denied equal rights with men. But how we addressed those issues (from 1960 until today) turned out to be our undoing.

The one clue that we might be headed in the wrong direction was our foreign policy, which had been influenced by neocons after World War II. America had fought the war in Korea, begun the war in Vietnam, and the military/CIA was stirring up trouble in many countries, especially South and Central America. We had become a global bully, and that has not stopped. The US government did not care about spreading democracy and human rights, as our record reveals. All we cared about was expanding

US hegemony, and dominating the global economy.

Lies from the national government and a lack of transparency began in the 1960s, with the coverup of the JFK assassination. Those lies would continue with the 9/11 commission (why did WTC Building 7 fall?), the Iraq invasion (based on so-called weapons of mass destruction), the 2020 presidential election (Biden received 81 million votes?), COVID (calling it a vaccine), and the Ukraine war (who really started it?).

I would also blame the government for the global warming/ climate change scam. Carbon makes up only .4% (less than 1%) of the atmosphere. The idea that man-made carbon pollution is causing climate change is propaganda. One thing we know is that excess carbon does not cause global cooling, which is what we are actually experiencing (this will become apparent by the end of the 2020s). Why the push for the control of carbon emissions (and dictating which industries are good for America?), which was popularized by Al Gore, a Democrat? Quite simply, it gives the government more influence and more power to wrest away individual sovereignty (freedom).

Everything began to change in the 1960s for the worse (with regard to our values). In fact, when we killed JFK, America lost its way, and our values have deteriorated ever since. From that point forward, we became a country that only had a thirst for power and money, and no longer cared about improving society. From that point forward, there was no more transparency from Washington, and the rule of law began to fade (the Constitution steadily lost its influence), and corruption began to expand in politics and our political institutions.

Feminism began to expand in the 1960s, bringing with it the concept of political correctness. Steadily, the value of meritocracy began to be marginalized as women demanded equality first and merit second. Slowly at first, but if you look back, you will see that deterioration of our meritocracy began to wane at that time.

Ironically, once meritocracy came under attack (and equality became the focus), our educational standards began to decline. As educational standards declined and feminism increased, the more ingrained became the distaste for the American values that reigned prior to the 1960s. Is there any question, that my analysis is correct? I don't think so. Was the shift away from meritocracy to equality (based on gender or race) a good choice? Not if you want humanity to thrive. Yes, if you want humanity to collapse.

From politically correct speech, we ended up with a political agenda that sought to transform America into something new. This was popularized by the Democratic Party, which steadily gave up on previously held American values (free speech and the right to have an opinion on any topic). This eventually led to CRT (critical race theory) being taught in schools. This is the theory that white supremacy is prevalent in society (a lie) and needs to be addressed. This theory instills racism and creates division, but Democrats don't seem to care. Sometimes I think Democrats just want to destroy the old America so that they can create a new America. As they will soon learn, the destruction will lead to the breakup of America, as their ideas are exposed as untenable.

Political correctness (now referred to as being woke) led to a plethora of statues being removed from public places. Even Thomas Jefferson's statue was removed in Philadelphia. Jefferson was perhaps the most influential Founding Father. He was canceled by the left for his moral flaws and his political incorrectness. At this time, anyone who is perceived to be politically incorrect can be canceled. It should be stated that it's not just morality that gets you canceled today, but political ideology. This is diabolical when America was based on liberty and the right to hold opposing political views. Prior to 1960, it was considered normal to hold opposing political views. Today, ironically, you can be killed in America for holding the wrong political views (this is not hyperbole!).

The agenda of defining political correctness has become so virulent that any supporter of Donald Trump has been deemed to be an extremist and a threat to democracy by many Democrats. Conservative political views are no longer acceptable in the opinion of those who are trying to create a new America. The irony is that those Democrats who are trying to create this new America are not being transparent about what they find deficient in these so-called extremists.

With the rise of politically correct speech came a gradual war on free speech. Most of the large social media companies banned a large array of voices that were deemed harmful to society. Those who deemed them harmful were mostly progressive voices that dominated these social media companies (many of which had a political agenda). And it wasn't only social media that had a war on free speech, it also carried over into the MSM (mainstream media), which began to limit what stories they would write about. Basically, the MSM began to self-censor themselves, and their writers, based on politics rather than the news. To say that the media became politicized is an understatement. Many people stopped watching/reading the MSM for this reason. Trump called it fake news, which was actually an understatement. It was worse than fake news. It was propaganda with an agenda to change America's values – to create a new America.

This steady rise of the politicization of how society should talk, think, and behave eventually made its way to government (national, state, and local). It was a stealth agenda to remake America into a new nation based on new values. Ironically, nobody debated the costs and benefits of such a radical transformation. Instead, we began to see changes, such as open borders during the Biden Administration (with busses ready to escort illegal migrants, and government programs ready to support these arrivals), sanctuary cities, leniency toward criminals, and defunding the police.

The 2020 January 6th riot in Washington D.C. was considered an insurrection by the Democrats, even though the rioters didn't have any weapons and were generally peaceful once they entered the Capitol building. Yet, the Washington D.C. courts treated them as criminals, with many of them waiting years for a trial (which is unconstitutional). It was the epitome of a corrupt legal system.

I'm not a supporter of Donald Trump, but the legal system treated him badly after the January 6th riot because of political motives by his opponents. I never thought in my lifetime that I would see the American legal system fall to this degree. How far the legal system has fallen is commiserate with how far the MSM, political system, and economic system have fallen. Our institutions have failed us.

America began to bifurcate in the 1960s, with one group holding onto the old values (based on the Constitution), and another group that wanted to go in a new direction (ripping up the Constitution). Sadly, that new direction was one of socialism and collectivism, which have never worked (and never will). This is the path of big government, whereby government elites dictate how individuals live their lives. It is a path of anti-liberty, anti-freedom. And, in fact, is a path that can never work because the human soul demands free will and will never be content to live under the auspices of government control.

Those who supported this move away from meritocracy and liberty were mostly Democrats (and some Independents). What they didn't realize was the problem wasn't meritocracy. Instead, it was a flawed economic system. Society wasn't smart enough to recognize that capitalism could be reformed to work for everyone without the need for government to take away our liberty.

The solution isn't big government, but economic reform. Hence, the progressives are fighting the wrong fight. This is starting to become obvious.

Because America could not figure out how to fix its problems (mostly inequality and lack of opportunity) through economic reforms (I include them in my new Constitution), both political parties became feckless. The Democrats wanted to limit liberty and allow government to dictate how we live our lives. For example, the Democrats are trying to push DEI (diversity, equity, and inclusion) onto employers (including government employers), which is the opposite of meritocracy. This is a form of indoctrination whereby we are told how to think, talk, and act. They also pushed ESG (environmental, social, and corporate governance) onto corporations. Another form of indoctrination pushed by the elites in Washington.

Ironically, while Democrats push political agendas for equity, equality, and the environment, they neglect the human rights of education (your zip code should not dictate the quality of your education), healthy food, and healthy water. Instead, they allow food companies to practically poison us and local municipalities to provide harmful water (do you drink out of your faucet?). Does the FDA work for citizens or the food and pharmaceutical companies? I think it is the latter. It's a travesty.

Healthcare is another mess, where our political leaders have failed us. Every advanced nation in the world offers public healthcare except the U.S. This should be a human right. In America, healthcare is treated as a profit-making enterprise and reflects our value of making money over human rights. The same is true of the drug/pharmaceutical industry, which should be non-profit and publicly supported for R&D.

Beginning in the 1960s, the government began to grow in size and influence. Today, it is a behemoth and continues to grow in size. Government growth led to the slippery slope of anti-liberty and political corruption. Why corruption? Because power corrupts, and power uses power to maintain power. A good example of this corruption was COVID. Even though the vaccine was not thoroughly tested and was experimental, Washington used its power to convince about two-thirds of the population to take the jab, threatening employees with their jobs if they refused. How many lies were spewed by the government regarding COVID?

What was grotesque about the COVID ordeal was how the media supported the government's efforts to get everyone vaccinated. The government used the media as a propaganda tool. Even when it became obvious that the vaccine did not prevent COVID, the media refused to say it. And when it became obvious the vaccine was dangerous (with many serious side effects), the media refused to say it. The media stopped doing their job and refused to report the news. The only people reporting the news were the alt-media, who were condemned as reporting misinformation.

The Democrats wanted to follow a path of collectivism, and the media was willing to support that effort. They called themselves progressives because collectivism has a bad connotation associated with communism. The progressives wanted to use a stealth approach to turning America into a country with new values. Unfortunately, their path was anti-liberty, which would never work. Plus, it was anti-capitalist to a large degree, and what economic alternative is there?

The Republicans weren't much better with their approach. They thought our economic system for free-market capitalism was just fine (as long as you limit regulations and taxes). This is total nonsense. Capitalism is severely flawed (which has now become obvious). Yes, it is the best economic system, but you need to regulate the flaws.

Flaw number one is that monopolies naturally form. We have huge companies such as Microsoft, Apple, Google, and Amazon. Yet, Washington does nothing to limit their power. Flaw number two is the rentier class, which generates its income from collecting rent or fees, yet provides no wealth effect (it's mostly unearned income). These are the landlords (who own property), insurance companies, banks, and financial services industries. These should all be non-profit or public enterprises. The rentier class and monopolies accumulate most of the wealth to the detriment of society. We need an economy that generates prosperity for all, not one that puts everyone in debt.

The Republicans do not acknowledge these flaws and will fight to keep monopolies and the rentiers in power. Why? Because they have become brainwashed into believing the free market should not be tampered with by government. This is why banks and insurance companies were bailed out in 2008, but consumers were not.

The other flaw the Republicans have is that they do not acknowledge that social problems are their responsibility to fix. They believe individuals are responsible for their actions and government programs should not be used to fix social problems. This is the reason many Democrats loathe Republicans. The Democrats are so angry at Republicans that they would rather destroy America than maintain the status quo.

In addition to the flaws of monopolies and the rentier class, our capitalist economic system has been running on debt since the 1980s (national debt consistently grows faster than GDP). We now have over $39T in national debt, and it is currently rising at over $1T per year. The national government interest payment for

2025 was around $1T, which is a huge number. The government has become trapped and must continue large deficits, or else the economy will contract (or potentially crash).

We have become trapped in a debt spiral. At some point in the near future, the Fed will need to monetize (purchase) this debt in a big way. Thus, the Fed will need to print digital money to purchase this debt and expand its balance sheet. This will cause inflation as the money supply grows rapidly. Plus, foreigners who hold our debt will sell it for fear that we will either default or the debt will decline in value.

The US economy has not only become debt-dependent for growth, but it is also trapped into using globalism and free trade. Since we no longer make the majority of items that we need, it will be very difficult to wean ourselves off of globalism. When you combine globalism with the flaws of capitalism I mentioned earlier, along with our dependence on debt for economic growth, we are in a very precarious situation.

So, not only is our political system broken, but so is our economic system. We have become imperiled. In fact, there is no way out, and we have reached the end of the U.S. era of global hegemony. All that is left is our fall, and I would submit that the nation will not be able to remain intact once this fall begins. So, we will start over. Not as a nation, but as a series of nations.

Thankfully, I am confident that the foundation of liberty, meritocracy, equality, and the rule of law will be used by the new countries that arise, and perhaps some of the ideas in my new Constitution will also be used.

I am confident that the insanity of this current era (since 1960) will be left behind. It won't fade easily in the blue states, but over time, individual freedom will regain its prominence as our overriding value. We will come to recognize that government exists to serve the individual and not the other way around. Moreover, that the duty of government is to ensure that individual sovereignty is not infringed.

INTRODUCTION

My political views have always deviated from the norm. I would not consider myself a radical, although I am a bit of a closet revolutionary. Not a violent revolutionary, but one who is open for radical change. I'm ready to support someone who comes up with grandiose ideas to solve our pressing problems. And since no one has emerged, I feel compelled to publish this new constitution.

I do have grandiose ideas, sme of which you will be exposed to if you read my constitution. However, I have never been interested in being a politician. I'm more of a philosopher than a politician. I would rather remain in the background of society. Sure, I don't mind writing books and sharing ideas, or even speaking publicly on occasion, but I don't want to lead.

It's not that I'm afraid to lead, it's more that I am aware that very few people care what I have to say. My views fit into a very narrow political platform, and perhaps I am wasting my time writing this constitution. An astrologer gave me a natal chart horoscope reading and the first words out of her mouth were, "I don't know what you're doing in this country. Nobody cares what you have to say." This was from a lady who I had never met before. So far, she has been right.

I've known intuitively that the astrologer was right. My ideas and beliefs are contrary to commonly accepted ideas. I often feel like a fish swimming upstream against the current. But I also know that my ideas are worth sharing.

I consider myself a utopian libertarian. I want to live in a country that honors my freedom, where everyone gets along with everyone else. Most people don't believe that is possible, so they settle for a less ambitious outcome. Once you give up on this ideal of a utopian libertarian society, you start down a path that only leads to bad outcomes. Many of those outcomes have led to the problems that we face today.

Today, society has fractured into many different groups that each want different things. What they all have in common is an aversion to an ambitious outcome. They are all content to settle for bad outcomes. In fact, our two most influential groups (the national political parties), have zero ambition for solving our problems. Instead, they have their own agendas for managing our problems.

We can summarize those agendas succinctly. The Democrats want to expand government programs (essentially, a call for bigger government) and use higher taxes to fund those programs. The Republicans want to limit the expansion of government programs (essentially, a call for smaller government) and maintain the status quo. Both of these groups do not have any real solutions, so all that will happen is that our problems will grow larger.

Eventually, in my opinion, the United States will break up into a series of smaller countries. If this does occur, then some of these new countries will likely try new forms of government and adopt new social structures. They will need to write new constitutions. Those new countries are the target audience for this book. I don't expect very many of my ideas to be incorporated into their new constitutions, but I thought I would help add to the discussion.

Everyone knows what utopia means. It is a society of perfection, where everyone is happy and has their needs met. While I don't believe we can achieve the ultimate utopian society, I do believe we can strive to achieve a society that embodies those ideals and values.

Libertarian has many definitions, and it means different

things to just about everyone. What most libertarians can agree on is that it is a philosophy that reveres free will and freedom and is skeptical of anything that limits that free will and freedom.

Most libertarians today are conservative. They want to have their freedom and are highly skeptical of big government allowing them that freedom. Worst case, they want government to stay exactly the same and not intrude any further on their freedoms. Best case, they want government to shrink and give them additional freedom.

The main difference between a utopian libertarian and a conservative libertarian is that utopian libertarians want to create a new society where everyone gets along and is treated fairly. Both are focused on individual freedom and small government, but the conservatives don't think it is possible to achieve utopia, so why try?

My philosophy is why not try? In fact, in my opinion, settling for less is unacceptable. I believe that it is our responsibility to try and create a society that is fair and just for all. Even our current constitution includes the high ideal of "all men are created equal."

I think our founding fathers had high aspirations of creating a society where people were treated equally. But that constitution was written during an era when there were few examples for them to borrow. Today, we have much more to draw from. I would say that today is ripe for starting over with a new constitution that can achieve our highest aspirations.

If we start over, with a new government structure and a new social structure, then there is no reason our aspirations have to settle for anything less than perfection. We can aspire to create a society that gives us the fulfillment that we all desire. That's what my new constitution attempts to achieve.

I know that people are generally risk-averse. For this reason, most of the new countries will write constitutions that they are familiar with. Perhaps, there will be one small country that attempts to solve our problems of inequality and lack of personal freedom. All we need is one pioneering country to show us the way.

As of today, it seems like a fantasy that a country would adopt utopian libertarian ideals. I actually think it is not only possible, but it is likely to occur. My background in metaphysics and spiritual philosophy gives me insight into the direction of humanity. I believe that a time is approaching when people will expect equality and personal liberty.

The expectation of equality and personal freedom is going to grow and grow until it is eventually manifested somewhere on this planet. Will it be during our lifetime? Perhaps, perhaps not. One can only hope. But I am optimistic about the future and expect to see a much more gentle humanity. I expect society to evolve until it matches the pure beauty of the planet..

Don Durrett 2/17/2026

Chapter One

A New Constitution

In the introduction, I gave you a short definition of how I would define a utopian libertarian. It is someone who wants to create a society that has a small government where individual freedom thrives, and everyone gets along in a fair and just manner.

This type of society is a radical departure from what exists today. For this reason, it could only occur by starting over and writing a new constitution. That would require a major undertaking, and I don't think it could be done on a national level. What is more likely to happen is that one of the states that secedes will attempt a radical departure from our current way of government and social structures.

It's almost certain that the first state to secede will not consider writing a constitution that exemplifies utopian libertarian ideals. However, one of the first few states to secede will likely form a government and social structure that is considerably different from what we have today. This departure from the past will introduce new ways of thinking about how to design a government and its supporting social structures.

After a few states secede and write new constitutions, we are likely to see more and more utopian libertarian ideals accepted. The reason why is because this is the form of government and social structure that is the most harmonious. Even if we do not achieve a utopian outcome, striving toward that goal will likely be attempted.

I know what you are thinking: utopian communities have already been tried and they always fail. My counter-argument is that this time is different. This time, they will be created out of necessity. This time, they will be created because humankind has evolved to the point that this form of social structure is demanded.

I don't want to go into detail on why our political and social structures are failing, but soon I expect the United States of America (U.S.) to break up into a series of countries. This constitution is meant to be read after the breakup begins, and something is needed to replace our old, failed social structures. I think we all recognize that our political and economic systems are broken, and that our social issues have grown into unsolvable problems.

*   *   *   *   *

So, what will we put in this new constitution? Some ideas can be taken from my book, Kern County: The Path to Secession and a New Constitution. In that book, I wrote a constitution that could form the basis of a new society. For this constitution, I will take some of those ideas and incorporate others. I will outline important ideas that I think will be useful once new countries begin to form new governments and new social structures.

In 1776, we had the Declaration of Independence. Something similar is going to be written for new countries out of necessity. No longer will our old way of life and old documents serve us. Something new will be needed.

Because change is likely to begin in small countries, they will not have the option of forming a large government. Most of these countries will be in no position to fund a large government. Thus, by default, they will need to organize a small government.

These new small countries and small governments will be ideal testing grounds for utopian libertarian ideas and values. I will outline one such possible constitution (the full constitution is included in the appendix).

* * * * *

Here are the initial passages in the new constitution:

Preamble

We hold these truths to be self-evident, that all humans are created equal, that they are endowed by their Creator with certain unalienable Rights, which among these are Life, Liberty, Justice, and the Sovereignty of the soul. To secure these God-given rights, Governments are instituted among People, deriving their just powers from the consent of the governed.

Declaration

We, the people, desire to form a country based on fairness, freedom, integrity, honor, justice, equality, and respect. The country will exist as a united whole that works together in harmony with cooperation. No one person or one group shall infringe upon the rights of others. Government shall remain limited in scope and size, with the citizens in charge of making all important decisions.

Guiding Principles

1. The liberty to be free without encumbrance.
2. Every human a respected sovereign being with equal human rights.
3. Opportunity for everyone, and no one deprived of education and basic necessities.
4. Service to the country and not service to one's self.

5. If a person cries out for help, the country will come to their aid.

6. Crime will not be tolerated.

7. Government kept to a minimal level.

8. Thrive and enjoy life.

9. Reach for your dreams, but you may have to work hard to achieve them.

10. Respect the environment, which includes earth, water, air, and all life forms.

Country Values

We are all neighbors and should treat each other fairly and kindly. We are all equals and should consider the humanity of our actions. Helping one another should be a priority for everyone. Any injustice, unfairness, or discrimination will not be tolerated.

Business Philosophy

Our goal is sustainability over growth, stability over complexity, quality of life over achievement. While competition is required in a capitalistic system, conflict and competition do not have to overshadow our humanity.

Chapter Two

Government and Laws

There will be no elected officials or elections. All government workers will be chosen in a similar process that is used today for jury selection. Thus, all government workers will be in service to the country for a short duration.

The selection pool of candidates to fill government positions will be created using the country's database. The database will contain a profile of each citizen. Each citizen will be responsible for filling out their profile on the country's website. These profiles will include each citizen's age, education, work experience, and essays that include detailed information of their proficiencies. Each citizen can also specify duties they would be interested in performing, positions they would be interested in fulfilling.

Government positions will last, at most, one year and, after you have served, you will be excused for at least one year.

Positions will be filled by selection committees comprised of currently serving government workers. These selection committees will be randomly generated based on existing similar positions.

There will be no individual leader of the country. Instead, there will be one group (the board of directors) that defines the required functions needed by the country. This group will be the most influential committee in the country. They can add new functions and remove others.

The board will be comprised of four men and four women. It will require a vote of five board members to make a change. Ten positions will be chosen annually by a randomly selected committee of existing high-level government positions. This selection committee will attempt to find the best ten candidates from the country. Two of the chosen candidates will be designated as first and second alternates, who can stand in for board member absences. These alternates can also serve as alternates for selection committees and arbitration panels.

Each year, the new board will have the ability to reverse any existing laws, rules, functions, plans, or taxes. This annual process creates a self-correcting mechanism.

Because the board and all government workers serve the people, the voice of the people is accomplished via vocal protests and the ballot box. If the voice of the people is not heard via protests, citizens can vote to overturn laws or decisions made by the board.

Citizens can march and protest against any decision made by the board. Protests do not require a permit and can occur on public property. People can march on public roads, but not on public highways.

Voting will occur on the first Tuesday in November if, during the year, ten percent of the voting-age population sign a petition to overturn an existing law. A majority vote is required to overturn a law. Digital signatures and digital voting are both acceptable. All citizens 21 years of age or older are eligible to vote. No voter registration is required.

In many respects, this form of government is risky because the board has nearly unlimited power to do what it wants for a single year. However, there is one way to limit their power, which is the constitution. The constitution requires that no one disrupt the harmony of the country. Anyone who disrupts the harmony is subject to banishment. This constitutional law could also be used to remove anyone from a government position, including board members.

While the country is based on the ideals of libertarian freedom, citizens do not have the right to disrupt its harmony. Conversely, if a citizen is not disrupting the harmony of the country, the government has no right to disrupt a citizen's harmony. It goes both ways. If everyone lives in harmony with one another, then everyone should have nearly complete freedom to do what they want.

The government shall only provide those services and functions that cannot be provided by private companies. This will include the following:

Laws and Functions (board of directors).

Administration (country website, citizen database, and ID cards).

Law Enforcement (arbitration panels, selection committees).

Business (regulations and licenses).

Healthcare (public option).

Housing (for the homeless).

Food (for those in need).

Revenue collection (taxes and fees).

Public safety (police and fire).

Money creation (fiat and crypto).

Voting (annual voting).

Most of these functions will be addressed in separate chapters.

There are several functions of the government that are not on this list. They include education, military, transportation, electrical, water, sewer, sanitation, roads, bridges, and the postal service. These functions will not be handled by the government. Most of these functions will be handled by local companies using government contracts, and the military by private militias.

The government will be kept as small as possible with no intention of growth. Those who work for the government will be paid their previous year's annual salary or a minimum wage if they were unemployed. Their previous position should be waiting for them after they return from public service. They can file a grievance with the arbitration panels if they have been discriminated against for missing work because of time spent in public service.

There will be two public safety functions that require positions that last longer than one year: the police and fire departments. To keep inefficiencies from occurring in these departments, these positions will last for five years, and the salaries will be kept low in the spirit of small government and low taxes. They will be treated as positions of service to the country in the spirit of volunteering. Every year, new police and fire department positions will be filled from a group of volunteers. If there are not enough volunteers, people who used to serve in these positions before will be asked to volunteer again. If someone enjoyed being a police officer or firefighter, they can put their name on a waiting list to volunteer.

Most government functions will require positions that are not difficult to learn. There will be a training program for each position. Some positions will require less than a day of training and others could take up to one month.

Ultimately, the board of directors is responsible for all functions of the government. It is their job to ensure that everything runs effectively and efficiently. They will have the power to make things happen as needed. They can add functions, change functions, and raise money as needed. There is no limitation placed on the board except to ensure that the harmony of the country is not disrupted.

If the harmony of the country is disrupted when the board convenes for the first time, then it is their responsibility to try to restore harmony. How they do that is up to them.

There shall be no judges or juries. Instead, there shall only be arbitration panels comprised of citizens. The board of directors will have the authority to assign or delegate to other committees the task of creating one-year arbitration panels. These panels will be responsible for enforcing the country's laws. They will have jurisdiction for all disputes, crimes, and misdemeanors. There can be several selection committees and several arbitration panels … whatever the board of directors deems necessary.

All selection committees and arbitration panels shall consist of four men and four women. If a member is absent, there will be alternates available. A majority vote will be used for decisions. The selection committee and arbitration panel members shall not use their religious beliefs for making government decisions. Instead, they will use the principles set forth in the constitution.

A member of the board, arbitration panel, or selection committee can be removed by an arbitration panel for unsuitable behavior. An arbitration decision in favor of removal can be appealed twice. If a citizen is removed from one of these groups, they will be replaced by an alternate. A new alternate shall be found using the same method used for finding alternates.

The board of directors has the authority to implement new laws, enter into trade agreements, and coin money. These laws and agreements can be rewritten and changed by the succeeding board of directors.

Any decision made by the board that has an impact on the country must be codified into law and posted on the country's website so that citizens have the right to review these decisions and, potentially, overturn them. Citizens can vote to overturn existing laws by a majority vote, but they cannot vote to implement new laws.

If citizens overturn a law, the current board of directors cannot create a similar law in the same year. If they do so, a citizen can file a grievance to revoke the law, which will go to an arbitration panel.

All arbitration decisions must be reached within three months of the filing. Decisions regarding disputes and crimes can be appealed twice. This can be considered a "three-strikes" process. After three derogatory decisions, it is final. The appeals process must be completed within three years of the first arbitration decision.

There is one exception to the "three-strikes" process. If new evidence is discovered, it can be presented to the board of directors, which can reinitiate a new arbitration case. If the evidence is compelling, there is no statute of limitations.

All arbitration hearings are to be recorded and made available as part of the public record on the country's website.

Citizenship is a privilege and not a right. Each citizen is responsible for themselves and must hold the values of the country. While each citizen will be respected as a sovereign soul, this does not give them the right to disturb the harmony of the country.

Instead of utilizing a long list of laws, the country will rely on a single framework of what is unacceptable behavior. This will be called "Disturbing the Harmony of the Country." This catch-all legal requirement will be implemented by the arbitration panels. While this catch-all requirement may seem counter to the country's credo of liberty and fairness, arbitration panels will be used to protect citizen's rights.

Anyone suspected of violating a law or Disturbing the Harmony of the Country can be reported to the police, who will inform the arbitration panels.

The purpose of the arbitration panels is to ensure that the guiding principles of the country shall not be infringed. Citizens can appeal decisions twice, so it will require three separate arbitration panels to all agree to impose a guilty verdict on a citizen. In the event this happens, citizens have the right to protest and make their voices heard. The board of directors can overturn an arbitration decision if they deem it inappropriate.

No standing country army will exist or be organized. Local militias are allowed to form on their own accord as long as their objective is for the defense and well-being of the country.

All citizens will be included in the government database. This database will include the profile of each citizen. It will include their picture, retinal scan, height, weight, eye color, home address, phone number, and email address. It will also include their education level, work history, and additional proficiencies. The government will issue ID cards, driver's licenses, and passports based on this information, which will be free to obtain by each citizen. The data must be updated at least every five years by each citizen.

A citizen can lose their citizenship if they have been found guilty of disturbing the harmony of the country and have been declared banished. Arbitration boards have the authority to issue, to those found guilty, sentences of either community service, fines, or banishment. If a citizen is banished, they will be given an escort to the border. If they come back, they will be banished to a remote location.

If a citizen or visitor is charged with disturbing the harmony of the country, they can be held by the police for a short duration while an arbitration panel makes a binding decision on either community service, fine, or banishment. The maximum period of incarceration will be three months.

Both a driver's license and vehicle registration will be free. No physical driver's license is required for driving. However, you must be 18 years old, pass an online test, and have an adult family member verify that you know how to drive. You can use your Government ID Card for identification. Vehicle registration can be done online, with the registration and license plate mailed to the citizen.

No toll roads will be allowed in the country. No cameras or electronic monitoring devices will be used to ticket vehicles for infractions on public roads or highways.

Vehicle insurance will be handled by one private company and will be nonprofit. Their contract will be renewed every three years. They will only insure damages to the vehicle or if the vehicle is stolen. The insurance company will be exempt from lawsuits. Citizens will be responsible for negligent driving and can be fined by arbitration panels or given community service. Driving privileges can also be suspended or revoked.

Morality will not be determined by statutes in the constitution. Morality will be the responsibility of parents and adults. Gun laws, illicit drug laws, gambling laws, and other morality-based laws will be determined by the board and not the constitution.

Local communities can protest the existence or non-existence of morality-based laws. If a local community wants to allow or disallow morality-based laws, they can petition the board to implement them. A community must show an overwhelming support or lack of support for a morality-based law in order for the board to add or remove it.

No smoking at indoor or outdoor public places or workplaces shall be allowed. Public parks are exempt, as well as domiciles where people live, which is considered to be personal private spaces. A personal private space can only be entered by the police with a probable-cause warrant.

Freedom will not be impinged upon without the guiding principles of the constitution taken into consideration. Spirituality and religion will be a personal matter and not infringed or discriminated against. However, if a religion is deemed counter to the guiding principles of the constitution, it will be banned.

Freedom of speech and a free press will be protected to the extent that it is not discriminatory or slanderous. All opinions are protected. Whistleblowers who report infractions will be protected.

All citizens have the right to file a grievance against a citizen, business, or government function. These shall be heard by an arbitration panel in a timely manner (within three months). If the grievance is identified as a frivolous complaint, the arbitration panel has the authority to side against the plaintiff.

Citizens can collect signatures from one-third of the electorate for a referendum to modify the constitution. These signatures can be collected electronically. A two-thirds electorate vote is required to pass the referendum.

Any form of advertising to enact or overturn laws is illegal. Any form of advertising that undermines the country's harmony is illegal.

All public land when the constitution is approved will transfer to the country's ownership. Private businesses can make requests to obtain public land for development. Arbitration panels will approve or deny and set the selling price for the parcel of land.

All private land that is not developed when the constitution is approved will transfer to the country's ownership. Before this transfer of ownership occurs, the private owners can request to develop the land into an operating business. They can also sell the land if they can find a party who will develop the land.

All water rights and minerals rights will be owned by the country. Private businesses can request leases for mining or access to water. Arbitration panels will determine the annual fees and renewal periods for these leases.

No licenses will be required for hunting and fishing. Hunting and fishing seasons and rules will be determined annually by the board of directors. Hunting and fishing areas will be included in their announcement, which will be posted on the country's website.

Public parks and community cleanliness will be maintained by both government employees and volunteers. Arbitration panels can also assign community service to offenders of disturbing the country's harmony to help with these duties. The board can also assign community service to teenagers if the country requires help with cleaning up a public area.

The owner of a property without a mortgage or lien shall not be evicted from his property unless an arbitration panel rules in favor of his/her banishment from the country. In the event of banishment, the offender will be paid the current market rate for their property.

A property owner or renter can be evicted from their place of residence after 60 days by an arbitration panel if a grievance is filed because of lack of payment on a mortgage, lien, or rent.

Chapter Three

TAXES AND MONEY

A flat tax of 10% on all income will be imposed on all citizens. Businesses will be exempt from income tax. This tax will be due on June 1 of each year. It will be paid to the revenue department. This department will have the authority to assign investigators for irregular tax filings or late payments, which can be reported to the arbitration panels. The board of directors will have the authority to raise the income tax rate above 10%. However, citizens can vote to overturn this increase.

A sales tax of 5% will be used for all transactions exchanging goods, except for certain exemptions. There will be exemptions for food, medicine, medical treatment, medical equipment, and personal property. The board of directors will have the authority to raise the sales tax rate. However, the citizens can overturn this increase.

There will be a 15% sales tax on overnight accommodations (room charges), gasoline, diesel, tobacco, alcohol, marijuana, sugar-flavored drinks, and fast food. The board of directors has the authority to add products to this list.

Inheritance, gifts, and personal property shall be exempt from taxation and not treated as income. Transactions of services shall be exempt from taxation. Transactions of real-estate property shall be exempt from taxation, but any profit for the seller will be treated as income. Gold, silver, and cryptocurrency shall be exempt from taxation.

All government income will come from income taxes, sales taxes, fees, and tariffs.

If the country runs a deficit, then taxes, fees, or tariffs can be raised. If there is a budget surplus, then taxes, fees, or tariffs can be lowered.

The government will not incur debt or borrow money. Ideally, the government will have a large amount of surplus reserves. These reserves can be held in various assets, including fiat currency, gold bullion, silver bullion, and cryptocurrency.

The board has the authority to implement tariffs if they deem them necessary. They have the authority to implement new taxes that are not forbidden in the constitution, although these can be reverted by subsequent boards or the voting public.

The department of revenue is responsible for collecting income taxes. They are also responsible for issuing new money. The country's fiat currency shall be gold-backed and convertible into gold. Growth in the money supply shall be determined by the board of directors.

A country cryptocurrency will also be issued. Businesses will have the right to transact in the fiat or cryptocurrencies of their choice. Income tax payments will be accepted in either the country's fiat currency or a specified cryptocurrency.

Chapter Four

Business and Trade

Business Philosophy

Our goal is sustainability over growth, stability over complexity, quality of life over achievement. While competition is required in a capitalistic system, conflict and competition do not have to overshadow our humanity.

* * * * *

Business has to be regulated because we know from experience that capitalism breeds inequities and monopolies. We also know that the pursuit of money can lead to dispassionate and inhumane practices.

While the guidelines, values, and business philosophy set forth in the constitution can help limit these adverse outcomes, we still need to incorporate regulations and laws to limit them further. Perhaps the one thing that lends itself to equality more any other in business is the pay structure.

The constitution compresses the pay structure to create more equality. The maximum difference in income from the top salary in a business to the bottom salary is 10 to 1. Moreover, any bonus pay or profit sharing will be the exact same for all employees. If the CEO is given a bonus, then all employees receive the same bonus amount. This is a team approach, where all citizens are given equal weight for the team result. This is how professional sports teams share their bonus money when they win a championship. Equal shares for each player.

Businesses are encouraged to give bonuses and share profits if the company is successful. This will improve morale and attract new employees. Because there are no shareholders or dividends, any profits accumulated can either be reinvested, saved, or distributed to employees and owners.

There will be no stock market, and companies operating in the country will not be allowed to be publicly traded. This prevents companies from splitting their loyalties between shareholders and employees. In our country, there will only be employees and business owners, and no shareholders.

If a company grows in size to the point that it is in a dominant position and prevents competition, the board of directors of the country has the power to split the company into two separate companies. If companies are found to collude for the purpose of both companies increasing their profits, they can be found to be disrupting the harmony of the community. The result can be fines, the firing of employees, and other judgments from an arbitration panel.

Trade unions will be illegal. With the compressed salary structure, there will be no reason for unions. This will create a better working relationship between employees and business owners.

Individuals can own multiple businesses, and they can sell these businesses for a profit. Business owners must report the profit from the sale of a business as income. They do not have to share the profit with the employees. This creates incentives for people to start their own businesses.

If the business has any cash or assets at the time of a business sale, those transfer to the buyer. If the owner wants to assume ownership of any cash or assets of the company prior to selling the business, then they must give the employees equal amounts. If the owner gets $1,000, then each employee receives $1,000.

Any injustice, unfairness, or discrimination can be reported to the arbitration panels by employees. Any business practices that are counter to the country's values can result in the loss of a business license.

An employee shall work a maximum of 30 hours per week, with overtime illegal. For those who want to work more hours, they can become a government volunteer or start a business. Business owners and volunteers are exempt from this restriction.

The minimum wage will be considered a living wage and set by the board of directors annually on January first of each year. Because the income of a business owner can only be ten times the lowest paid employee, the starting pay for many businesses will be higher than the minimum wage.

Banks, insurance companies, and other finance companies shall all be nonprofit. Some businesses will need to follow the few regulations that are issued by the country. Most businesses are self-regulating and subject to the loss of their business license if they do not honor the guiding principles of the country.

Businesses that build things, such as houses, buildings, roads, and bridges will need to follow the country codes. Doctors and other professional positions, such as CPAs and lawyers will be required to have a license. The country will provide a list of professions that require a license.

Another regulatory requirement is labeling. All products sold must be labeled, except for personal property, which is exempt. The labeling requirements are defined by the board.

If there is a budget deficit and additional revenue is necessary, the board of directors can implement tariffs. However, this is not recommended, and free trade is preferable.

If there is a trade deficit with another country, the recommended solution is to require that country to make a percentage of their product in our country. If they are a publicly traded company, they then can use a local business to make their product.

A business license is free and can be obtained online. There are no business reporting requirements, although financial statements must be kept for ten years in the event of an audit. A business owner found to be in violation of maintaining financial records can lose their privilege to hold a business license.

There shall be one national holiday each month. On these holidays, no one shall work except the following: hospital staff, police and fire departments, and travel-related industries. The board of directors can modify this list as needed.

Full-time employees will receive a minimum of 4 weeks' paid vacation. Part-time employees will receive a minimum of 2 weeks' paid vacation. Mothers will receive 12 weeks of paid maternity leave after giving birth, and then 4 weeks of paid maternity leave in years 2 and 3.

Chapter Five

HEALTHCARE

The first priority of healthcare is to remove all profitability and make all healthcare-related industries as nonprofit companies. This includes hospitals, doctors, dentists, optometrists, and all healthcare-related fields.

The second priority is to provide a multi-tiered approach. The first tier will be private healthcare using private sector health insurance. The second tier will be private healthcare using holistic practitioners for citizens who are self-insured. The third tier will be the public option, where healthcare (hospitals, doctors, dentists, optometrists, etc.) is a single-payer system run by the country. Citizens are only charged what they can afford, with a maximum of 3% of their income for the calendar year.

The single-payer system will be operated by a nonprofit company that is given a contract that is renewed every three years. All employees of the single-payer company will be paid by salary. This will keep billing and budgeting simple.

The bill for any single-payer service should be kept to a minimum amount of information. All it needs to contain is the citizen's name, citizen's ID, provider's name, service provided, and any charges due. Because all single-payer employees are on salary, only the single-payer needs to be paid for a service.

The single-payer company has only two streams of income: one from the government and one from payments for services rendered.

Electronic medical records will be available for citizens to monitor online. These records will be secured from unauthorized access. All three tiers will share the same medical records database, which will be maintained and secured by a private company.

The medical records database can be used for research and reporting purposes, with the identities of the citizens excluded. This will provide useful information to the populace, such as how many people were recently admitted with the flu and their age groups.

The goal of healthcare is to provide a country service and not for individuals to become enriched. Those who provide service for the country, such as healthcare workers, police and fire department workers, need to recognize that these are professions of service and not enrichment. If you want to be enriched, then start a business that enriches the country, which can then be sold at a profit that goes to the owner.

The single-payer company will likely be the largest employer in the country and the largest cost for the country. To reduce the healthcare cost of the country, the single-payer company should implement efforts to promote well-being using prevention and awareness programs. Moreover, the country should consider good health to be a priority.

Fees charged to patients will be subject to review by arbitration panels for potential excessive charges. This can be requested by patients, healthcare practitioners, hospitals, or the single-payer company. Health and nutrition shall be taught in high school for at least one year. The focus of this education will be on preventing disease and staying healthy.

Medical doctors shall be required to obtain and maintain a medical license, whereas holistic practitioners shall be self-regulated. Pharmaceutical drugs and health supplements shall be self-regulated. However, any citizen can submit a complaint to the arbitration panels to ban a drug or supplement. Companies found to be negligent can lose their business license.

A website for the country will be created to share information about local medical doctors, holistic practitioners, pharmaceutical drugs, and supplements. The website shall be open to the public for posting and sharing information.

Post America: A New Consititution

Chapter Six

Education

Education shall be the highest priority of the country. All children will get the opportunity for a high-quality education. Teachers and principals will be reviewed annually for performance. Poor performance reviews will lead to terminations.

Education will be free for students from pre-school through college. Each school will provide day-care for any student in need. Schools will not be public institutions. Instead, they will be run by nonprofit private companies, with three-year contracts.

Students and parents can choose which school to attend. There will be an online option for students who choose to study from home. They can switch schools at any time. However, problem students can be relegated to specific schools to ensure high-quality education for all.

Students must pass an exam at the 6th grade and 8th grade level to move forward. They must also pass an exam to graduate from high school to become eligible for a college education.

Any student who fails their exam at the 6th grade or 8th grade level can attend summer school and attempt to pass the test a second time. If they do not pass, then they must repeat that grade level.

The option for free college education will mostly be performed online, with face-to-face educational settings used out of necessity.

Each school will have the option to experiment with different curriculums and teaching methods. It is recommended that schools offer diverse teaching methodologies so that students can decide which school is right for them. A cookie-cutter approach is not advised, where each school is teaching the same curriculum and teaching methods.

Before college, it is also recommended that students are exposed to a wide array of subjects instead of a narrow set of traditional subjects. They should be allowed to learn about music, art, dance, meditation, spiritual practices, health and nutrition, politics, religion, science, philosophy, numerology, astrology, astronomy, software applications, computer programming, technology, finance, cooking, and handyman skills. They should be taught to think critically and not just how to memorize. They should have opinions about what they have learned.

Ideally, students should be able to choose what they want to learn from a wide array of options. Online courses now make this possible. The only courses that should be required are those that teach students how to read and write, along with basic math skills. Every student should be adept at reading and writing. The exit exams at the end of the 6th grade, 8th grade, and high school should focus on reading and writing. Anyone who can read and write proficiently can learn nearly any subject.

If 95% of the population will never use math beyond basic computations, why should it be a requirement in high school? Why are other subjects neglected and math emphasized? The focus of education should be to provide learning that students will use throughout their lives.

Once a student turns 16, they should have the option to learn a trade or technical skill. This option should remain for any citizen at any point in their lifetime. Hands-on training should be provided for free to all citizens who show an interest. The cost is part of the country's free education options.

Chapter Seven

HOUSING AND FOOD

Public housing centers will be separated into different areas, such as short-term homeless, long-term homeless, disabled, mentally ill, and elderly. With the availability of public housing, there will be no need for sleeping on the streets. While some citizens may prefer a nomadic lifestyle, it will be required for them to sleep at the public housing centers if they are homeless. This is for the safety and harmony of the community.

The public housing centers for the short-term homeless will be designed to provide a temporary refuge and not a permanent community. It will only provide the bare necessities and not attempt to create a high quality of life or sustainable living arrangement. The food menu will be austere and the amenities just as austere. Conversely, it should provide free counseling, job training, and job placement. Those residing in these centers should be given help to get back on their feet.

The public housing centers for the long-term homeless will be a permanent community and provide a home for those who have not been able to assimilate into society. These communities will likely require extra police surveillance to ensure public safety. They will also need to have a public food center and a public health clinic that these community members can share.

* * * * *

Any house that has not been lived in for 12 months must be put on the market for sale or sold at auction. Any house on the market for more than six months must be sold at auction. All houses offered at auction must have an open house for three days prior to the auction. All houses up for auction will be sold to the highest bidder without a minimum price.

Single-family houses must not be owned for the purpose of rental income. All single-family rentals must be sold or put up for auction within six months after the constitution is approved. The value of all single-family houses will be appraised when the constitution is approved. From that point forward they can only appreciate in value as determined by arbitration panels. If you want to sell your house, an arbitration panel will determine its price.

Multi-unit housing will be allowed as rental properties, although they must be nonprofit. All multi-unit housing rental rates will be determined annually by arbitration panels, based on the financial situation of the owner and the current market rates. If an owner sells a multi-unit housing property, the profit will be considered income and taxed at the current income tax rate.

It's possible for a private business to own more than one multi-unit housing complex. However, owners of multi-unit housing will not be allowed to become enriched by charging high rent. The rental rates paid by tenants will be based on the financial health of the owners. If the owners have no debt on the property, then rates can be lowered.

* * * * *

No country currency or cryptocurrency shall be given to those in need by the government. Instead, assistance will be given directly to those in need. Public food centers will be supported by the government. Free transportation to these centers will be available to the public.

All food products sold in retail stores must have labels that include the ingredients. No GMO products can be grown or sold in the country. No pharmaceutical drugs can be given to animals intended for food production unless administered by a veterinarian for an illness. No herbicides can be used within the country. The board of directors can use its discretion to create additional laws that protect the public's health.

All products sold must be labeled, except for personal property, which is exempt. The labeling requirements are defined by the board.

Citizens are encouraged to have their own gardens and grow their own food. They are allowed to sell their food at local farmers markets or in front of their homes. These home-grown products will be considered to be personal property and not subject to income tax.

Selling home-grown food will supplement incomes, leading to more self-sufficiency for citizens. It will also help improve the health of citizens and lower the cost of healthcare through better nutrition.

Chapter Eight

Immigration and Visitors

Anyone is allowed to visit the country, and visitors have the same rights as citizens. There are no border guards or immigration officials. No passports or visas are required to visit. Visitors who want to stay for longer than one year must find employment, in which case they will be given a work visa. Visitors who do not find employment must leave after one year. The waiting period for a return visit can be determined by the board of directors.

Anyone found to be a visitor who has extended their visit beyond one year will be banished immediately. These violations will be treated seriously by the country because there will be many people who want to live in a harmonious, utopian-like community. Violators will lose their opportunity for a return visit and placed in a database. No business will be allowed to hire anyone in this database. Plus, anyone abetting a violator will be fined.

Businesses are allowed to hire non-citizens to come and work in the country. These non-citizens will be given work visas, and their immediate family can come with them. Any non-citizens found working without a work visa will be banished. Knowingly hiring a non-citizen without a work visa is illegal.

Visitors (non-citizens) can request citizenship using several methods. The first is that, after working for five years (aggregate time), a visitor can apply for citizenship. The second way is through a family member. A citizen can request that a family member be given citizenship. An arbitration panel will decide the outcome. The third way is through immigration requests from non-citizens.

The board of directors can determine how many immigrants are allowed each year. They can also set a list of criteria required for immigrants. It is recommended that immigrants fill roles that are lacking or under-represented in the country, such as highly skilled labor.

Visitors (non-citizens) can start and own their own businesses. If a visitor starts a new business, they must submit their financial records for the first five years. If the business is not generating sufficient revenue, then it can be at risk of losing its business license. If this occurs, the visitor will have to leave the country.

Citizens and visitors will not be held by the police without a charge. All will have a hearing by an arbitration panel in a timely manner. There shall not be a death penalty.

No citizen or visitor will be subject to unlawful searches or seizures. A person's possessions, be they things, records, or ideas, shall not be taken without due process of an arbitration panel. A person's physical and mental health shall be protected.

No citizen or visitor will be compelled to be a witness or provide information in a legal matter. Each citizen or visitor will have the right to make their own choices and decisions, unless those choices and decisions impact the harmony of the community.

Afterword

I'm writing this update in 2026, although I wrote a large portion of the constitution in 2014 and 2018. I don't know when the country will begin to break up or if a new country will incorporate some of the ideas in this book. However, I thought I would share some of my thoughts about why I wrote it, just in case it actually happens.

Ever since I was young, I questioned our social, political, and business institutions. I grew up in California in the 1960s and 1970s. At that time, there were a lot of positives about society, but that wasn't enough to satisfy me. I always wanted more and demanded more from society. Not necessarily for myself, but for society as a whole.

My biggest problem was the hypocrisy. It was very clear to me, early on, that opportunity was skewed toward the rich. Those who went to good schools clearly had more opportunities to succeed. And those who were unfortunate to have been born into poverty or the lower class were faced with challenges that many Americans were not.

I might have been okay with it if our political leaders had been transparent about the inequalities and were trying to fix the problem, but they weren't. Instead, we were fed propaganda that everyone was on a level playing field and had equal opportunity. We were told that all you had to do was work hard and you could obtain the American Dream.

What was even worse, since no one would even acknowledge the discrepancies in inequality, nothing was being done to fix the problem. That was fifty years ago, and nothing has changed. In fact, it has gotten worse. Today, education has withered in low-income school districts, especially in large urban cities. Many students in America today do not even learn how to read and write. It's a tragedy, yet nothing is being done or even discussed by our politicians and corporate leaders.

The other part of society that I thought was abhorrent was the lack of humanity and a dominant business culture. When teenagers graduate from high school, they are practically fed to the wolves. You have few choices. Basically, you have three. You can go to work, join the military, or go to college.

If you decide to go to college, you get to incur an enormous amount of debt. Plus, you have to learn what they offer. It's very much a cookie-cutter type of education where they put everyone into groups and then shuttle them into existing positions. It is very dehumanizing.

Then, when you begin working, the pay is usually terrible for at least 80% of first-time workers. Most people are forced to incur debt and live paycheck to paycheck. It is often a very tedious and unrewarding career. And in America, the amount of time off is limited, so you end up giving most of your life to a job that unfulfilling.

I was subjected to this lifestyle, and I know there is a better way. Calling this the greatest country in the world because about 15% of the population is affluent and successful is naive from my viewpoint. Yes, there are a lot of successful people, but there are also a lot of unsuccessful people who are struggling. The dichotomy is too great to ignore.

For decades, we Americans ignored this dichotomy and pretended this is as good as it gets. However, as we smiled and pretended that life was good, we could see society degrading. The 1% continued to become even more prosperous and successful, but the middle class began to shrink. Problems mounted and intensified.

As a nation, we were forced to acknowledge that times had changed and not for the better. Our way of life was challenged on many fronts, and many of the facts that we tried to deny and ignore were surfacing. The homeless problem began to explode. The cost of education was becoming a burden too high to pay. The cost of rent and housing was becoming unaffordable. The steady demise was clear for all to see.

Watching this slow decay of our so-called values of equality and fairness made me question the viability and longevity of America. I could foresee the eventual failure of solving our biggest problems. I think I've always questioned the ability to solve our big problems using our current political system.

By the time I was thirty, I had decided that there were no political solutions to our biggest problems. From my perspective, it was too late, and we had fallen too far. I came to this conclusion because our political system had become fractured beyond repair. That fracture is now apparent to everyone as the nation has split apart into fractious groups, mainly two: conservatives and liberals.

I can now understand why the Civil War occurred in the 1800s. If we didn't have the Internet and television to keep us informed, we might be engaged today in another civil war. Or, at the very least, a great deal of violence and loss of life.

America has split into groups that no longer trust each other. We no longer get our news and information from the same sources. Instead, we prefer to get our information from sources that already agree with us. The division has become so inflamed that violence between these groups has already started. Conversations between these groups often become shouting matches with palpable vitriol.

Once I realized that political solutions were no longer possible for solving our biggest problems, I realized that all I could do was wait. I called this waiting period "easy street." This is what we have today, but it is a time that is quickly fading. Today, society is muddling along with a semblance of normalcy, where the stores are full, and you can still get whatever you need fairly quickly and easily.

Today, if I need something, I either go to a nearby store, or I log in to my computer and have it delivered. Easy peasy. I can't think of a single product that is hard to get or is expensive. Raw walnuts, at around $12 per pound, is probably the only item that I buy on a regular basis that I would consider expensive. My grocery bill averages about $75 per week, but that's not going to last much longer.

I equate this period to the movie Terminator, where Sarah Connor waits for Judgment Day. Perhaps that is a bit of hyperbole, but America, as we know it, is headed for a trying period from which it will not recover. At least, that is my take. America, as we know it, will be no more, and we will have to start over. Under this scenario, the possibility of states forming a new country is quite likely.

While education, opportunity, and inequality are focal points of my criticism, our corporate structures and government power are a close second. I have always cherished my freedom and liberty. I feel that they are God-given rights for humanity, and I respect the U.S. Constitution for emphasizing these rights. However, what I have experienced in my lifetime is a government and corporate power structure that seems intent on limiting our freedom and liberty.

These power structures are often referred to as "The Man." Jack Black, in the movie, School of Rock, did an excellent job of explaining to young kids how rock 'n roll was one way to "stick it to the man." The "man" is the iconic representation of who control things and forces us to abide. The "man" strips us of our freedom and demands our allegiance.

Does the "man" exist today? Sure, it does. Power has become highly concentrated in both corporations and government institutions. Many people believe that corporations are more powerful than government institutions and, in fact, control the government. That is a possibility.

One thing that is prevalent today is the incessant collection of private citizen information by both corporations and government. I think we can assume that the details of our lives exist on a myriad of computers and that anyone with enough access can collect that information. Recently, Congress held hearings about this collection of information, but nothing was done to stop it.

Corporations have become so powerful, that they have had laws passed that legally allow them to collect information about our lives. Currently, our ISP (Internet Service Provider) can save information about every web page that we visit. Then they can legally sell this information to other companies. This is the reason why, when you do an Internet search or visit a web page, shortly after that, you get an advertisement related to that information. But this type of information collecting is only the tip of the iceberg.

The power of corporations has become unbridled. Today, employees are already being chipped, while the government looks the other way. Most of these chips are injected using a needle and are the size of a grain of rice. There are several companies, today, that either requires chipping or offer chipping. Those that offer chipping put subtle pressure on their employees to be a team player. This is only going to continue.

The next things that are important to society are what impact the quality of our life. This would include the quality of the environment, such as clean air and clean water, along with a nutritional food supply that is non-toxic and non-harmful.

Other things that impact the quality of our life include our work life and transportation systems, shipping providers, along with access and distribution of information via the Internet.

In my envisioned constitution, I banned corporations, publicly traded companies, and trade unions. I replaced them with a close relationship between business owners and workers. I also reduced the work week. These changes should increase the quality of life substantially.

So, those are the issues that I think are the most important in society. First, I want to live in a society that is equal and just, where everyone gets along regardless of differences. Second, I want government and corporations not to impinge on my freedom and liberty.

Some say that this is a utopian fantasy, but I say, it is possible. And the constitution I have written shows how it can be done, or at least attempted. Perhaps not in a country of 350 million people, but it could work in a smaller country of perhaps five million or less. Ideally, I would like to see it tried in a country of one million or less. If it works there, then it could be tried on a larger scale.

✻   ✻   ✻   ✻   ✻

I think that today, most people know the problems we face and recognize that radical changes are necessary. I say, let's start over and solve them with a new approach. Let's analyze each problem and find the best solution. That was my approach when I wrote my constitution.

I never had an idea to write a new constitution prior to 2014. In fact, it may never have happened, except that a friend of mine had a dream in which I wrote a best-selling book about state secession. At first, I rejected the idea, but then, I had an idea of Kern County (where I lived) seceding from California and forming a new country called Isabella. Once I had that idea, I decided to write a book about it.

When I began writing the constitution for Isabella, it was actually pretty easy and did not take very long. The constitution for Post America was also easy to write. I think that is from my lifelong interest in politics, business, and social structures. I have always been interested in these subjects.

When I was in college, my political science teacher asked me if my major was political science because I asked a lot of questions. It would have been a good career for me, but there was one problem. I disagreed with both party platforms, and I was cynical of the political system. My disagreements with both parties were so strong that becoming involved with either political party was not an option for me. I decided that I would rather be a spectator and watch it degrade and eventually fail.

I wrote a book called The Demise of America after the financial crisis of 2007. In that book, I wrote the obituary for America and explained what happened and what caused our downfall. It was an easy book for me to write because I have always been a bit of an American historian of the modern era. I wrote the first draft in only a month or two.

I have never considered myself a great writer, but I do think I am a big thinker and consider myself a spiritual philosopher. I have written in several genres. I started out writing new age spiritual books, and that is probably my best work. It is also where I have produced the most material. After I got bored writing new age books, I started branching out into other genres. I became an expert in investing in gold and silver mining stocks, so I wrote a book on that subject. Then I wrote The Demise of America, which is a political/historical book. Finally, I ended up writing a book on health. I'm sure there will be a few more books and perhaps more genres to come.

I feel like I am a quasi-expert in several different fields. I have an M.B.A. and understand business, corporate organizations, and corporate cultures. I'm well-versed in metaphysics, politics, health, and investing. I've worked in IT fields for 20 years as a computer programmer and technical analyst. I think it was my diverse knowledge that allowed me to consider writing a new constitution.

Appendix: New Constitution

Preamble

We hold these truths to be self-evident, that all humans are created equal, that they are endowed by their Creator with certain unalienable Rights, which among these are Life, Liberty, Justice, and the Sovereignty of the soul. To secure these God-given rights, Governments are instituted among People, deriving their just powers from the consent of the governed.

Declaration

We the people desire to form a country based on fairness, freedom, integrity, honor, justice, equality, and respect. The country will exist as a united whole that works together in harmony with cooperation. No one person or one group shall infringe upon the rights of others. Government shall remain limited in scope and size, with the citizens in charge of making all important decisions.

Guiding Principles

1. The liberty to be free without encumbrance.
2. Every human a respected sovereign being with equal human rights.
3. Opportunity for everyone, and no one deprived of education and basic necessities.
4. Service to the country and not service to one's self.
5. If a person cries out for help, the country will come to their aid.
6. Crime will not be tolerated.
7. Government kept to a minimal level.

8. Thrive and enjoy life.

9. Reach for your dreams, but you may have to work hard to achieve them.

10. Respect the environment, which includes earth, water, air, and all life forms.

Country Values

We are all neighbors and should treat each other fairly and kindly. We are all equals and should consider the humanity of our actions. Helping one another should be a priority for everyone. Any injustice, unfairness, or discrimination will not be tolerated.

Business Philosophy

Our goal is sustainability over growth, stability over complexity, quality of life over achievement. While competition is required in a capitalistic system, conflict and competition do not have to overshadow our humanity.

Article I

Section 1

There will be no elected officials or elections. All government workers will be chosen from a selection pool using the profile web page of each citizen. Each citizen will be responsible for filling out their profile and maintaining it on the country's website. These profiles will include each citizen's education, work experience, and essays that include detailed information of their proficiencies. Each citizen can specify positions they would be interested in performing. They can volunteer for jobs or be assigned. Medical exemptions for government service will be available for the disabled.

A citizen's previous position will be waiting for them after they return from public service. They can file a grievance with the arbitration panels if they have been discriminated against for missing time at work.

Article I

Section 2

Government positions will last at most one year, and after you have served, you will be excused for at least one year. Positions will be filled by selection committees comprised of currently serving government workers. These selection committees will be randomly generated based on existing similar positions.

There will be no individual leader of the country. Instead, there will be one group that defines the requirements needed by the country. This group will be comprised of four men and four women and will be called the board of directors, or the board. It will require the same vote from five board members to make a decision. All votes made by board members will be made public to the country on the day of a vote.

Ten positions will be chosen annually by a randomly selected committee of existing high-level government positions. This selection committee will attempt to find the best ten candidates from the country. Two of the chosen candidates will be designated as first and second alternates, who can stand-in for board member absences. These alternates can also serve as alternates for selection committees and arbitration panels.

A member of the board, arbitration panel, or selection committee can be removed by an arbitration panel for unsuitable behavior. An arbitration decision in favor of a removal can be appealed twice. If a citizen is removed from one of these groups, they will be replaced by an alternate. A new alternate shall be found using the same method for finding alternates.

Article I

Section 3

There shall be no judges or juries. Instead, there shall only be arbitration panels comprised of citizens. The board of directors will have the authority to assign or delegate to other committees, the task of creating 1-year arbitration panels for all disputes, crimes, and misdemeanors. There can be several selection committees and several arbitration panels ... whatever the board of directors deems necessary.

Article I

Section 4

The board of directors has the authority to implement new laws, enter into trade agreements, and coin money. However, these laws and agreements can be re-written and changed by the succeeding board of directors. Moreover, the citizens can vote to overturn existing laws by a majority vote. There shall be no citizen voting to implement new laws, only to overturn existing laws.

Any decision made by the board that has an impact on the country must be codified into law so that citizens have the right to review these decisions and potentially overturn them.

If citizens overturn a law, the current board of directors cannot create a similar law in the same year. If they do so, a citizen can file a grievance to revoke the law, which will go to an arbitration panel.

Citizens can march and protest against any decision made by the board. Protests do not require a permit and can occur on public property. People can march on public roads, but not on public highways.

Article I

Section 5

Voting will occur on the 1st Tuesday in November if during the year 10% of the voter age population signs a petition to overturn an existing law. A majority vote is required to overturn a law. Digital signatures and digital voting are both acceptable. All citizens 21 years of age or older are eligible to vote. No voter registration is required.

Article I

Section 6

All arbitration decisions must be reached within 3 months of the filing. Decisions regarding disputes and crimes can be appealed twice. This can be considered a three strikes process. After three derogatory decisions, it is final. The appeals process must be completed within three years of the first arbitration decision. There is one exception to the three strikes process. If new evidence is discovered, it can be presented to the board of directors, which can reinitiate a new arbitration case. If the evidence is compelling, there is no statute of limitations.

All arbitration hearings are to be recorded and made available as part of the public record on the country's website.

Article I

Section 7

All selection committees and arbitration panels shall consist of four men and four women. If a member is absent, there will be alternates available. A majority vote will be used for decisions. The selection committee and arbitration panel members shall not use their religious beliefs for making government decisions. Instead, they will use the principles set forth in the constitution.

Article II

Section 1

Citizenship is a privilege and not a right. Each citizen is responsible for themselves and must hold the values of the country. While each citizen will be respected as a sovereign soul, this does not give them the right to disturb the harmony of the country.

Article II

Section 2

Instead of utilizing a series of laws, the country will rely on a single framework of what is unacceptable behavior. This will be called Disturbing the Harmony of the Country. This catch-all legal requirement will be implemented by the arbitration panels. While this may seem counter to the country's credo of fairness, arbitration panels will ensure it is not abused. The guiding principles of the country shall not be infringed.

Article II

Section 3

No standing army will exist or be organized. Local militias are allowed to form of their own accord, as long as their objective is for the defense and well-being of the country. The only long-term government employees will be police and firefighters. These positions will only last for five years, although citizens can be re-assigned to these positions.

Anyone suspected of violating a law or Disturbing the Harmony of the Country can be reported to the police, who will inform the arbitration panels.

There shall be no secondary government police force or intelligence organizations. There shall be no sharing of personal information, except for those authorized to access medical records or validate a job applicant.

Article II

Section 4

All citizens will be included in the government database. This database will include the profile of each citizen. It will include their picture, retinal scan, address, phone number, email, height, weight, and eye color. It will also include their education level, work history, and additional proficiencies. The government will issue ID cards and passports based on this information, which will be free to obtain by each citizen. The data must be updated at least every five years.

Article II

Section 5

A citizen can lose their citizenship if they have been found guilty of disturbing the harmony of the country and have been declared banished. Arbitration boards have the authority to issue verdicts of either community service, fines, or banishment. If a citizen is banished, they will be given an escort to the border. If they come back, they will be banished to a remote location. (Article I, Section 6 allows a citizen to appeal an arbitration panel decision twice before the decision is final).

If a citizen or visitor is charged with disturbing the harmony of the country, they can be held by the police for a short duration while an arbitration panel makes a decision on either banishment, community service, or a fine. The maximum duration period will be 3 months.

Article III

Section 1

The department of revenue is responsible for collecting income taxes. They are also responsible for issuing new money. The country's fiat currency shall be gold-backed and convertible into gold. Growth in the money supply shall be determined by the board of directors.

A country cryptocurrency will also be issued. Businesses will have the right to transact in the fiat or cryptocurrencies of their choice. Income tax payments will be accepted in either the country fiat currency or a specified cryptocurrency.

Article III

Section 2

Banks, insurance companies, and other finance companies shall all be nonprofit. There shall be no stock market, nor any publicly traded companies operating in the country. Only private businesses will be allowed to operate.

Article III

Section 3

Business shall use a maximum 10 to 1 pay scale, whereby the top paid employee is paid no more than 10 times the lowest paid. Any bonus pay or profit sharing will be the exact same for all employees. If a business is sold, the profit is considered income for the owner. They do not have to share the profit with the employees. This creates incentives for people to start their own businesses. There are no limitations on how many businesses a citizen can own.

If the business has any cash or assets, those transfer to the buyer. The owner of a business can only have an annual income of ten times (10x) the lowest paid employee. If the owner wants to assume ownership of any cash or assets of the company, they must give the employees equal amounts. If the owner gets $1,000, then each employee receives $1,000.

Article III

Section 4

Unions shall be illegal for both private and public employees. There shall be no collective bargaining. Any injustice, unfairness, or discrimination can be reported to the arbitration panels. Any business practices that are counter to the country's values can result in the loss of a business license.

Article III

Section 5

Inheritance, gifts, and personal property shall be exempt from taxation and not treated as income. Transactions of services shall be exempt from taxation. Transactions of real-estate property shall be exempt from taxation, but any profit for the seller will be treated as income. Gold, silver, and cryptocurrency shall be exempt from taxation.

Article III

Section 6

A flat tax of 10% on all income will be imposed on all citizens. Businesses will be exempt from income tax. This tax will be due June 1st. It will be paid to the revenue department. This department will have the authority to assign investigators for irregular tax filings or late payments, which can be reported to the arbitration panels. The board of directors will have the authority to raise the income tax rate above 10%. However, citizens can vote to overturn this increase (refer to Article I, Section 4).

Article III

Section 7

A sales tax of 5% will be used for all transactions exchanging goods. There will be exemptions for food, medicine, medical treatment, medical equipment, and personal property. The board of directors will have the authority to raise the sales tax rate. However, the citizens can overturn this increase (refer to Article I, Section 4).

Article III

Section 8

There will be a 15% sales tax on overnight accommodations (room charges), gasoline, diesel, tobacco, alcohol, marijuana, sugar-flavored drinks, and fast food. The board of directors has the authority to add products to this list.

Article III

Section 9

An employee shall work a maximum of 30 hours per week, with overtime illegal. For those who want to work more hours, they can become a government volunteer or start a business. Business owners and volunteers are exempt from this restriction.

Article III

Section 10

The minimum wage will be considered a living wage, and set by the board of directors annually on January 1st. Because the income of a business owner can only be 10x the lowest paid employee, the starting pay for many businesses will be higher than the minimum wage.

Article III

Section 11

Both a driver's license and vehicle registration will be free. No physical driver's license is required for driving. However, you must be 18 years old, pass an online test, and have an adult family member verify that you know how to drive. You can use your Government ID Card for identification. Vehicle registration can be done online, with the registration and license plate mailed to the citizen.

Article III

Section 12

If there is a budget deficit and additional revenue is necessary, the board of directors can raise the income tax rate, sales tax rate, fees, or implement tariffs. Any of these new laws can be overturned by a citizen vote (refer to Article I, Section 4).

The government will not incur debt or borrow money. Ideally, the government will have a large amount of surplus reserves. These reserves can be held in various assets, including fiat currency, gold bullion, silver bullion, and cryptocurrency.

If there is a trade deficit with another country, the recommended solution is to require that country to make a percentage of their product in our country.

Article III

Section 13

No toll roads will be allowed in the country. No cameras or electronic monitoring devices will be used to ticket vehicles for infractions on public roads or highways.

Article III

Section 14

Vehicle insurance will be handled by one private company and will be nonprofit. Their contract will be renewed every 3 years. They will only insure damages to the vehicle or if the vehicle is stolen. The insurance company will be exempt from lawsuits. Citizens will be responsible for negligent driving and can be fined by arbitration panels or given community service. Driving privileges can also be suspended or revoked.

Article III

Section 15

The owner of a property without a mortgage or lien shall not be evicted from his property unless an arbitration panel rules in favor of his/her banishment from the country. In the event of banishment, the offender will be paid the current market rate for their property.

A property owner or renter can be evicted from their place of residence after 60 days by an arbitration panel if a grievance is filed because of lack of payment on a mortgage, lien, or rent.

Article III

Section 16

Citizens are encouraged to have their own gardens and grow their own food. They are allowed to sell their food at local farmer's markets or in front of their homes. These home-grown products will be considered to be personal property and not subject to income tax.

Article III

Section 17

If a company grows in size to the point that it is in a dominant position and prevents competition, the board has the power to split the company into two separate companies. If companies are found to collude for the purpose of both companies increasing their profits, they can be found to be disrupting the harmony of the community. The result can be fines, the firing of employees, and other judgments from an arbitration panel.

Article IV

Section 1

No country currency or cryptocurrency shall be given to those in need by the government. Instead, assistance will be given directly to those in need. Public housing centers, public food centers, public healthcare centers, and public job training centers will be supported by the government. Free transportation to these centers will be available to the public.

Article IV

Section 2

Public housing centers will be separated into different groupings, such as the short-term homeless, long-term homeless, disabled, mentally ill, and elderly. With the availability of public housing, there will be no need for sleeping on the streets. While some citizens may prefer this lifestyle, it will be required for them to sleep at the public housing centers if they are homeless.

Article IV

Section 3

The public housing centers for short-term homeless will be designed to provide a temporary refuge and not a permanent community. It will only provide the bare necessities and not attempt to create a high quality of life or sustainable living arrangements. The food menu will be austere and the amenities just as austere. Conversely, it should provide free counseling, job training, and job placement. Those residing in these centers should be given help to get back on their feet.

Article IV

Section 4

Any house that has not been lived in for 12 months must be put on the market for sale or sold at auction. Any house on the market for more than 6 months must be sold at auction. All houses offered at auction must have an open house for 3 days prior to the auction. All houses up for auction will be sold at the highest bid without a minimum price.

Article IV

Section 5

Single-family houses must not be owned for rental income. All single-family rentals must be sold or put up for auction within 6 months after the constitution is approved. The value of all single-family houses will be appraised when the constitution is approved. From that point forward they can only appreciate in value as determined by arbitration panels. If you want to sell your house, an arbitration panel will determine its price.

Article IV

Section 6

Multi-unit housing will be allowed as rental properties, although they must be nonprofit. All multi-unit housing rental rates will be determined annually by arbitration panels, based on the financial situation of the owner and the current market rates. If an owner sells a multi-unit housing property, the profit will be considered income.

It's possible for a private business to own more than one multi-unit housing complex. However, owners of multi-unit housing will not be allowed to become enriched by charging high rent. The rental rates paid by tenants will be based on the financial health of the owners. If the owners have no debt on the property, then rates can be lowered.

Article IV

Section 7

Healthcare shall be a three-tier system. The first tier will be private healthcare using licensed professionals. The second tier will be private healthcare using holistic practitioners. The third tier will be the public option, where healthcare (all doctors, dentists, optometrists, etc.) is a single payer system run by the country. Citizens are only charged what they can afford, with a maximum of 3% of their income for the calendar year.

All healthcare-related businesses shall be nonprofit. Doctors' salaries can be a maximum of 10 times the lowest salary in the organization. Fees charged to patients will be subject to review by arbitration panels for potential excessive charges, which can be requested by patients. Health and nutrition shall be taught in high school for at least a single year. The focus of this education will be on preventing disease and staying healthy.

Article IV

Section 8

Medical doctors shall require a medical license, whereas holistic practitioners shall be self-regulated. Pharmaceutical drugs and health supplements shall be self-regulated. However, any citizen can submit a complaint to the arbitration panels to ban a drug or supplement. A country website to share information about local medical doctors, holistic practitioners, pharmaceutical drugs, and supplements shall be created and open to the public for posting information.

Article V

Section 1

The postal service, cable service, garbage service, phone service, water service, sewer service, maintenance of roads and bridges, electrical service, and natural gas service will be private and awarded to the lowest bidder every 3 years. The board of directors can add services to this list if it is in the interest of the country.

Article V

Section 2

Anyone is allowed to visit the country. There are no border guards or immigration officials. No passports or visas are required to visit. Visitors who want to stay for longer than one year must find employment, in which case they will be given a work visa. Visitors who do not find employment must leave after one year. The waiting period for a return visit can be determined by the board of directors.

Anyone found to be a visitor who has extended their visit beyond one year will be banished immediately. These violations will be treated seriously by the country because there will be many people who want to live in a utopian environment. Violators will lose their opportunity for a return visit and placed in a database. No business will be allowed to hire anyone in the database. Plus, anyone abetting a violator will be fined.

Businesses are allowed to hire non-citizens to come and work. These non-citizens will be given work visas, and their immediate family can come with them. Any non-citizens found working without a work visa will be banished. Knowingly hiring a non-citizen without a work visa is illegal. If a non-citizen works in the country for five years, they can request citizenship. Their time worked does not have to be contiguous.

Non-citizens can start and own their own businesses. If a non-citizen starts a new business, they must submit their financial records for the first five years. If the business is not generating sufficient revenue, then it can be at risk of losing its business license. If this occurs, then the visitor will have to leave the country.

Article V

Section 3

There are few business regulations other than following the
country's building codes and honoring the principles of the country.
A business license is free and can be obtained online. There are
no reporting requirements, although financial statements must be
kept for 10 years in the event of an audit. A business owner found
to be in violation of maintaining financial records can lose their
privilege to hold a business license.

Article V

Section 4

All food products sold in retail stores must have labels that include
the ingredients. No GMO products can be grown or sold in the
country. No pharmaceutical drugs can be given to animals intended
for food production unless administered by a veterinarian for an
illness. No herbicides can be used within a country. The board
of directors can use its discretion to create additional laws that
protect the public's health safety.

All products sold must be labeled, except for personal property,
which is exempt. The labeling requirements are defined by the
board.

Article V

Section 5

Morality will not be determined by statutes in the constitution.
Morality will be the responsibility of parents and adults. Gun laws,
illicit drug laws, gambling laws, and other morality-based laws
will be determined by the board and not the constitution.

Local communities can protest the existence or non-existence of morality-based laws. If a local community wants to allow or disallow morality-based laws, they can petition the board to implement them. A community must show an overwhelming support or lack of support for the board to add or remove a morality-based law.

Article V

Section 6

No smoking at indoor or outdoor public places or workplaces shall be allowed. Public parks are exempt, as well as where people live, which is considered to be personal private spaces. A personal private space can only be entered by the police with a probable cause warrant.

Article V

Section 7

Any form of advertising to enact or overturn laws is illegal. Any form of advertising that undermines the country's harmony is illegal.

Article VI

Section 1

Education shall be the highest priority of the country. Children will get the opportunity for a high-quality education. Teachers and principals will be reviewed annually for performance. Poor performance reviews will lead to terminations.

Article VI

Section 2

Education will be free for students from pre-school through college. Each school will provide day-care for any student in need. Schools will not be public institutions. Instead, they will be run by nonprofit private companies, with three-year contracts.

Article VI

Section 3

Students and parents can choose which school to attend. There will be an online option for students who choose to study from home. They can switch schools at any time. However, problem students can be relegated to specific schools to ensure high-quality education for all.

Article VI

Section 4

Students must pass an exam at the 6th grade and 8th grade level to move forward. They must also pass an exam to graduate from high school to become eligible for a college education.

Any student who fails their exam at the 6th grade or 8th grade level, can attend summer school and attempt to pass the test. If they do not pass, then they must repeat that grade level.

Article VI

Section 5

The option for free college education will mostly be performed online, with face to face educational settings used out of necessity.

Article VII

Section 1

All public land when the constitution is approved will transfer to the country's ownership. Private businesses can make requests to obtain public land for development. Arbitration panels will approve or deny and set the selling price for the parcel of land.

All private land that is not developed will transfer to the country's ownership. Before this transfer of ownership occurs, the private owners can make a request to develop the land into an operating business. They can also sell the land if they can find a party who will develop the land.

Article VII

Section 2

All water rights and minerals rights will be owned by the country. Private businesses can request leases for mining or access to water. Arbitration panels will determine the annual fees and renewal periods for these leases.

Article VII

Section 3

No licenses will be required for hunting and fishing. Hunting and fishing seasons and rules will be determined annually by the board of directors. Hunting and fishing areas will be included in their announcement, which will be posted on the country's website.

Article VII

Section 4

Public parks and community cleanliness will be maintained by both government employees and volunteers. Arbitration panels can also assign community service to offenders of disturbing the country's harmony to help with these duties.

The board of directors can assign community service to teenagers if the country requires help with cleaning up a public area.

Bill of Rights: Amendments

Amendment 1

Freedom will not be impinged without the guiding principles of the constitution taken into consideration.

Amendment 2

Spirituality and religion will be a personal matter and not infringed or discriminated against. However, if a religion is deemed counter to the guiding principles of the constitution, it will be banned.

Amendment 3

Freedom of speech and a free press will be protected to the extent that it is not discriminatory or slanderous. All opinions are protected.

Amendment 4

Citizens and visitors will not be held without a charge. All will have a hearing by an arbitration panel in a timely manner. There shall not be a death penalty.

Amendment 5

No citizen or visitor will be subject to unlawful searches or seizures. A person's possessions, be they things, records, or ideas, shall not be taken without due process of an arbitration panel. A person's physical and mental health shall be protected.

Amendment 6

Any form of discrimination is deemed illegal. Impacted parties can seek compensation from arbitration panels.

Amendment 7

Whistleblowers who report infractions will be protected. No citizen or visitor will be compelled to be a witness or provide information in a legal matter.

Amendment 8

All citizens have the right to file a grievance against a citizen, business, or government function. This shall be heard by an arbitration panel in a timely manner (within 3 months). If the grievance is identified as a frivolous complaint, the arbitration panel has the authority to side against the plaintiff.

Amendment 9

Citizens can collect signatures from one-third of the electorate for a referendum to modify the constitution. These signatures can be collected electronically. A two-thirds electorate vote is required to pass the referendum.

Amendment 10

There shall be one national holiday each month. On these holidays, no one shall work except the following: hospital staff, police and fire departments, and travel-related industries. The board of directors can modify this list as needed.

Amendment 11

Full-time employees will receive a minimum of 4 weeks' paid vacation. Part-time employees will receive a minimum of 2 weeks' paid vacation. Mothers will receive 12 weeks of paid maternity leave after giving birth, and then 4 weeks of paid maternity leave in years 2 and 3.

www.ingramcontent.com/pod-product-compliance
Lightning Source LLC
Chambersburg PA
CBHW072154020426
42334CB00018B/2001